For Colleen — from Bowmans
Ma---
for being a new ---
MORROW

LINDA'S INDIAN HOME

MARTHA FERGUSON McKEOWN

ILLUSTRATED WITH PHOTOGRAPHS BY ARCHIE W. McKEOWN

BINFORDS & MORT *Publishers*, Portland, Oregon

FOR OUR GRANDDAUGHTER, DAVINNE

Printed by Metropolitan Press,
Portland, Oregon, U. S. A.
Copyright, 1956
by Martha Ferguson McKeown
L. C. Catalog Card Number: 56-8826
All Rights Reserved
First Edition

TO THE YOUNG READER

This is a picture story of a little Indian girl who lives at Celilo Falls in the great gorge of the Columbia River. The story tells about the life and customs of Linda and her tribe, the Wy-ams, at the age-old fishery.

It is a story of Indian faces—faces filled with goodness and kindness and love. I hope it answers the question of the little boy who asked me, "If I met an Indian Chief would he try to kill me?"

THE AUTHOR.

LINDA'S INDIAN HOME

Linda is a little Indian girl. She lives in the Chief's house beside Celilo Falls, on the Columbia River in Oregon. Linda and her mother, Josephine, live with the Chief and his wife.

The Chief's wife, Flora, made this cradle board for Linda. It is called a "skene." Linda's skene is hung with rattles made of early-day trading shells. These trading shells are sea shells. The Indians used them instead of money. The Chief says that Canoe Indians brought these sea shells to Celilo Falls more than a hundred years ago.

The rattle hoop is made from a bent limb of a tree. It keeps the baby's head from getting bumped if the skene tips over. A skene keeps a baby from crawling into the fire. It keeps a baby from falling into the river. It is a safe place to put Linda when her mother is not holding Linda in her arms.

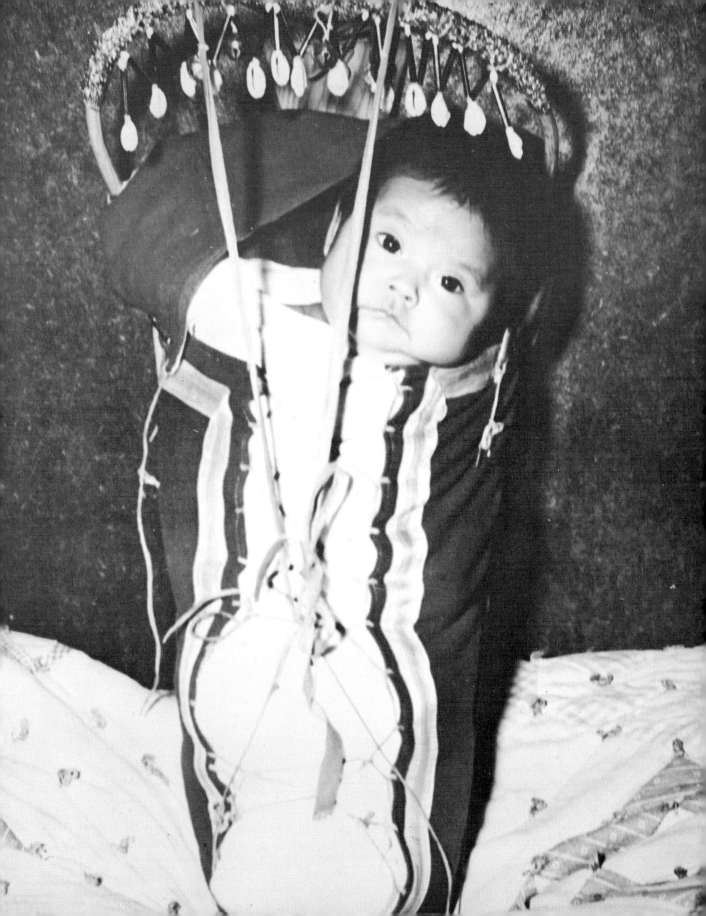

Linda's mother often takes her out of the skene. Then Linda laughs and kicks and stretches her arms and legs.

A skene is a little home. An Indian baby lives in it for the first few months of its life. The back of the skene is made from a flat board. It is narrow at the foot and wider at the shoulders.

The front of Linda's skene is made of heavy cloth. So is the big hood that can be pulled down over her head on cold days.

Before the white men came with goods to trade for furs and fish, the Indian women made skenes of buckskin from tanned deer hides. They packed moss inside the skenes to keep their babies warm and dry. They made baby clothes of soft, unsmoked fawn skins.

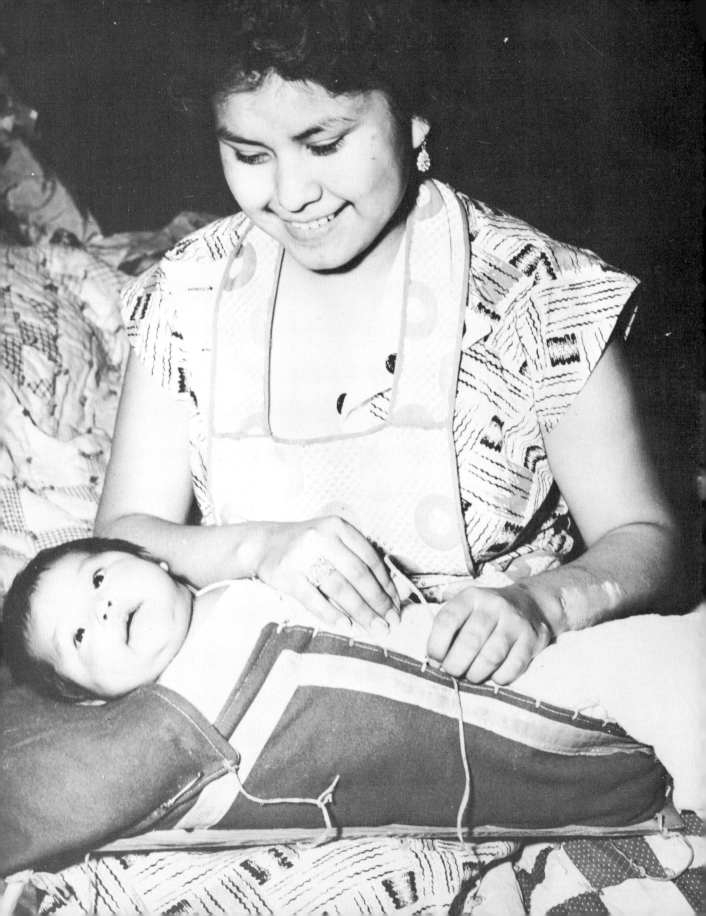

Linda's mother is lacing Linda back into her skene with a long lacing made of buckskin. She uses just one lace on the skene.

When she made Linda's skene, she used an old stone needle to make holes in the front of the heavy cloth. She tied a buckskin lace on each side, at the top. She made little loops clear down the front and tied the laces together at the bottom.

Now she has tied her buckskin lacing in the top hole. She can quickly pull it through the loops and tie it at the bottom. She does not have to put it through each one of the tiny holes in the skene.

Linda is sucking on a pacifier that her mother bought in a store. She is quiet because she is happy. She does not know that she cannot get milk out of a plastic pacifier!

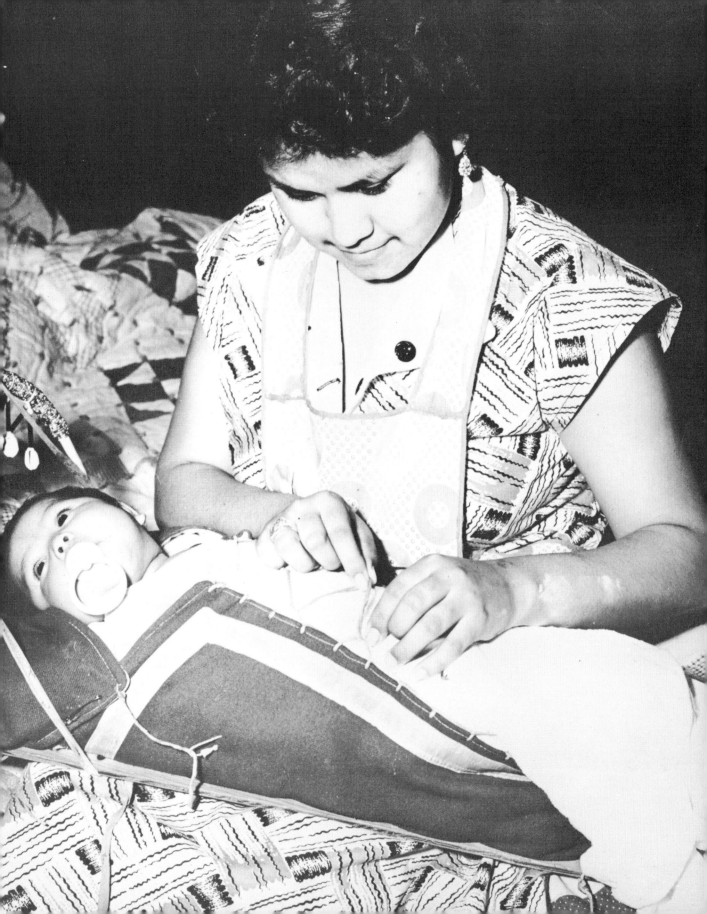

Long ago, Indian mothers gave their babies dried eels' tails to suck while they were lacing them into their skenes.

Eels are long and thin. They pull themselves along the rocks by holding on with little suction cups. They have seven holes on the sides of their heads. The Indians say that their God, the Almighty, uses these seven holes to count the days of the week.

Eels taste like fish. These eels are going to be made into eel soup. Each summer, Indian mothers dig wild roots. They wash and peel them and dry them in the sun. Then they cook them with dried eels or salmon heads to make soup. Wild roots are Indian vegetables.

This little boy and his mother are "comers." They have come to the village from their home on a reservation. They have come to trade two deer skins for a big basket of dried eels.

The mother is telling her baby a story about the eels. The Indian name for eel is "as-sim."

The as-sims creep along the rocks. They are the same color as the rocks. They try to slip past the village. But the Indian fishermen watch for the as-sims. When they see them inching along the edge of the water, they reach down and pull them off the rocks. They bring them to the village where they are dried and stored until winter.

Then the mothers make eel soup. And the babies eat so much eel soup they grow right out of their skenes.

When Linda was a tiny baby she didn't like to live in her skene. The day she came home from the hospital, where she was born, she looked like this.

Her mother was not pleased to have her act this way. But the Chief and his wife said, "Do not worry. She will learn."

And Linda has learned to live in her skene. Now she is quiet for hours, in her skene propped up against the wall. If she starts to cry, her mother moves her over in front of the window. Then Linda can watch the Columbia River. It goes tumbling over the Falls into the deep, white rapids below.

"Wauna" is the Indian name for the Columbia River. Wauna is a beautiful word. It means "the River."

The Indians all love to listen to the music of the crashing river as it goes tumbling down over the big rocks at Celilo Falls. And they love to listen to the echoes as they come singing back from the high cliffs on either side. These Indians are the Wy-ams. "Wy-am" means the echo of the water against the rocks at the Falls.

These Indians are called Fish Indians. That is because they make their living here fishing for salmon. They build these platforms out over the water. They tie themselves onto the platforms. Then they hold their dip nets down in the water and wait for the big, silver salmon to swim into them.

The salmon have reached the Falls. Linda's father has caught a big salmon in his dip net. He is pulling it up out of the water. He is dragging the heavy net up onto the platform. He will hit the salmon on the head with a big stick to kill it.

He traded salmon for lumber to build this fine platform. He traded salmon for the material to make his big dip net. He traded salmon for the heavy rope that he has tied around his waist. If he should tumble into the swift water below the Falls, he would use the rope to pull himself back to the fishing rocks.

At noon Linda's father will take his fish to the Chief's drying shack, where the women clean and dry the fish. He will eat his lunch there. Then he will hurry back to the fishing rocks again.

The Wy-am fathers come home every day to have dinner with their families. And they take time to hold and talk to their little boys and girls.

This is Jimmy George holding his little son, LeRoy. Jimmy George is a very wise man. He is the youngest man on the Wy-am Tribal Council. He meets with Chief Thompson and the other wise old men in the village. He can tell you how the Wy-ams have lived on these rocks since the beginning of time.

Jimmy George loves this place. He is thankful to God for letting him live here. He calls God, "the Almighty." He wants to do everything he can to please the Almighty.

Little Chief is six years old and he isn't nearly so big as this big salmon!

Columbia River salmon often weigh more than fifty pounds each. No wonder the River Indians call the salmon "The Great Food."

Each spring they hold a salmon feast to thank the Almighty for sending them the salmon. No one in the village ever eats spring salmon until the village has held its great feast of Thanksgiving.

The Wy-am men and women wear their hair in long braids to show the Almighty that they have not changed in any way since He placed them on these rocks to fish.

Mrs. Thompson is very worried because Little Chief will have to cut his braids before he goes to the "white man's school." She is afraid a short-haired man cannot catch big salmon.

Chief Thompson is sitting in front of his summer home. He is looking out at the deep, wide river crashing down over the Falls. He is worried.

He believes that the Almighty has sent these small salmon to punish his people. He believes that the Almighty is angry because the younger Indians are trying to learn the white man's ways.

All of the Wy-am families have winter and summer homes. The winter homes are small. Cold winds blow down the deep gorge of the Columbia River. It does not take so much wood to heat a little winter home.

A summer home must be very large. It must be made with an open side toward the river so that the clean, hot winds will blow in and help dry the fish. This is why the Wy-ams call their summer homes their dry shacks.

Each spring the men move all of their fish nets to the dry shacks. When they are not fishing they are mending their nets or making new ones.

Chief Thompson is teaching Max Boise to make a net. Max is a mute. No matter how hard he tries he cannot talk like other boys and girls. But the Chief knows that Max will always have plenty to eat as long as he can catch salmon.

Each spring the women move the beds and dishes into the low, wooden dry shacks beside the Falls. They sleep by the fish while the fish are drying. They get up in the night and turn them to keep them from spoiling. They put wood on the fires while the fish are smoking. They guard them from robbers. Fish mean more than money to the River Indians.

Chief Thompson's dry shack is his summer home. The front is open to the river. The three other sides are made of boards. The dry shack does not have any windows in it. The long back wall is lined with the tule mats. Tule mats are woven from the tall rushes that grow in damp, shady places near the river.

The only door is on the southeast corner. It swings back and forth on the leather hinges. The Chief has painted the door salmon pink. He uses this door when he goes out to read the morning sky for messages from the Almighty.

Chief Thompson was born in a house made like this one. It belonged to his uncle, Chief Stoecketli, and stood on the point at the head of Celilo Falls. Lewis and Clark came into Chief Stoecketli's home to buy fish and smoke the pipe of peace in 1806.

Lewis and Clark were the first white men to write about the Indians living here. They found the Indians living in a long, low building made of hand-split boards and tule mats.

From the first salmon of the spring until after the last salmon of the fall, Chief Thompson keeps watch over the fishing rocks. When he is not fishing for salmon, he sits in front of his dry shack and looks out at Celilo Falls.

His old fishing place on Chief's Island is called Long Pole. That is because he always uses a very long pole on his dip net. All of the River Indians have their own fishing places. When an Indian boy is big enough to hold a dip net, his father takes him out to their family fishing place. These places have always been passed down from a father to his son. The Wy-ams believe it is wrong for an Indian to fish in another man's place.

But when strange Indians come to the fishing rocks they do not follow these rules. They have not learned their lessons from Chief Thompson and the other old River Indians. They do not listen when he tells them they must not fish at night. And they do not listen when he says part of the fish must be allowed to go up the river to lay their eggs in the gravel beds far above the Falls.

Each spring and each fall the salmon come up the Columbia River. Each spring and each fall the fishermen catch the salmon in their big round dip nets. Each spring and each fall the women work in the dry shacks, cutting and drying the salmon. Then, when the cold winds blow down from the great snow-covered mountains, the fishermen will move their families back into the tight little houses under the cliff. And all of the River People will have plenty of food for the winter.

Minnie Charlie Johnlee is sitting in the front of her dry shack. Her dry shack is right next to the Chief's. A whole row of little dry shacks like this one is on the high bank beside the Falls. When the women look up from cutting fish, at the front of the dry shacks, they can see their fishermen out on the rocks.

Racks for drying fish take the place of a front wall in Chief Thompson's dry shack. Each part of a salmon has a special place on the dry racks.

Each part of a salmon has a special name. Bright pink slices are cut away from the backbone. They are the "a-wiss." They are the very best pieces of all. But no part of a salmon is ever wasted by the River Indians.

This picture shows the salmon heads. "Lok-lok" is the Indian name for the salmon head. "See-wee" is the Indian name for the backbone. Lok-lok and see-wee are both dried and cooked with roots to make fish soup.

Dry racks are placed north and south so the clean air from the river will blow between them. There is a little fire trench under each dry rack. Little smoky fires are made from green wood, in the trenches. Fir and pine branches do not make good fires for smoking salmon. Willow and maple are always best.

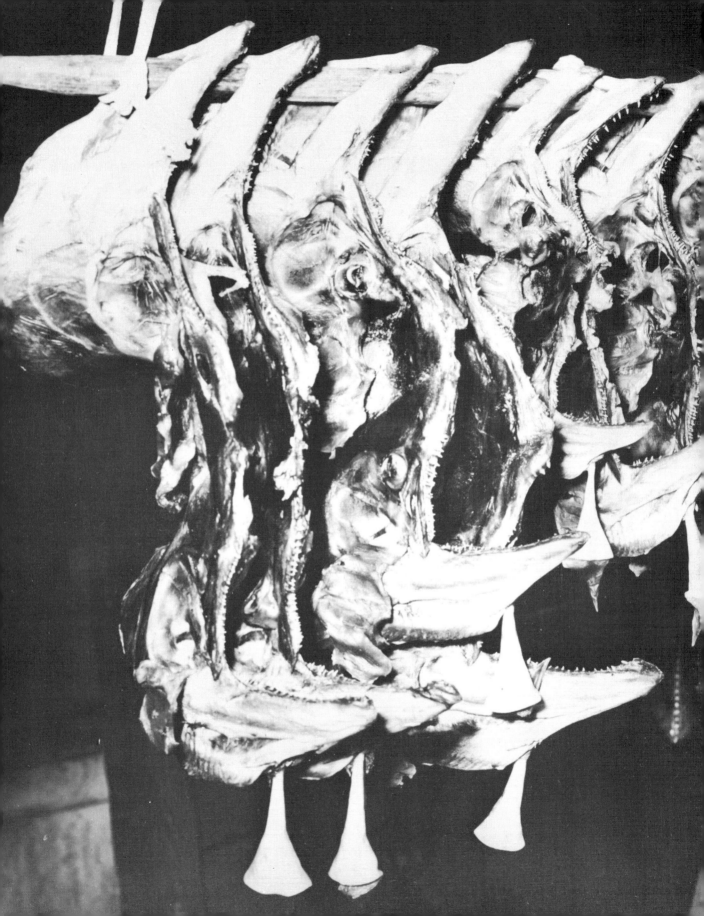

Linda's cousin thinks he is too big to stay in his skene. This morning, when his mother started to pull his skene around him, he kicked his legs. He waved his arms. She said, "Little man, we will see if you are big enough to leave your skene today."

All during the salmon season, the families live in the dry shacks. They sleep and eat in the big, dark room behind the dry racks. They visit while they are getting their food for the winter. This is the happiest time of all for the River Indians.

Each night, Cousin Tuckta and his mother and father sleep with their heads toward the long back wall of the Chief's dry shack. They store their things there, in big, shawl-wrapped bundles. At night the blankets are spread on the hard dirt floor. In the daytime the blankets are folded back against the wall to keep them clean. Indians sit on blanket rolls instead of chairs when they live in a dry shack.

Tuckta is unhappy. His mother has placed him out of the way in this dishpan of water because Tuckta has not learned to mind.

When his mother put him on the blanket beside Linda, he did not play with Linda. He crawled up to the front of the dry shack. Then his mother had to stop cutting fish and carry him back.

Tuckta is a stubborn little boy. He would not stay on the blanket. He scattered the little green sticks that his mother had put under a dry rack for smoking salmon. Then he reached up and pulled down a big roll of salmon eggs that Mrs. Thompson was saving for the Chief's dinner.

Tuckta is smiling again. His father has come back from the Falls. Mrs. Thompson is filling a big bowl with fish stew for Tuckta's father.

Tuckta knows that his father will sit on the blankets and talk to him while he is eating the stew. Tuckta knows that his father will take time to hold him in his arms. He will show Tuckta the great salmon he caught this morning on Chief's Island, far out in the Columbia River.

Tuckta's father is a reservation Indian. His winter home is at Warm Springs, many miles from the river. Tuckta's mother is Chief Thompson's great-niece. When they were married, Chief Thompson gave them a place to spread their blankets in his dry shack. He told Tuckta's father to fish on Chief's Island with the rest of the Wy-ams.

Tuckta's father pays Chief Thompson in fish for the use of his fishing place and dry shack.

In the old days, all young Indian boys learned to stalk deer with their bows and arrows. Deer were used for food and for clothing. Now only a few of the River Indians have money enough to buy cars and guns and go on long hunting trips.

A friendly hunter gave Mrs. Thompson these deer hides. For many days she soaked them in water. She scraped all the hair away with a dull, stone knife. She softened the hides with a mixture of animal tissue and water. Now she is softening the hides by pulling them back and forth in her hands. Soon she will smoke and tan them over a slow fire of green wood. Then she will make moccasins for the Chief and Linda.

"Mowitch" is the Indian name for deer. The mowitch are used both for food and clothing. Deer meat is called "venison." Venison is another Great Food.

The Indians believe that at the time of Creation, the Almighty made four Great Foods—the salmon, the venison, the roots and the berries.

Before the fields were fenced and plowed, the River Indians used to dig and eat seventeen different food roots. They ate them as we eat flour and potatoes and vegetables.

These four women have walked many, many miles searching for roots to eat and to dry. All they found was one little bed of "kouse," a plump black root. They have traded salmon for potatoes, to eat with the kouse.

The younger Indians who own cars or horses still go up into the mountains to pick huckleberries. When they get there they like to build tepees like this one.

When young pine trees grow close together, the sun cannot get down through them and they drop their lower limbs. The Indian men cut and trim these tall, slender trees for tepee poles. Then they carry them to the place where they want to build a tepee.

The men tie the poles together near one end. They stand them up and spread them apart. Each pole is braced against another at the top. These crossed poles are slanted out to make a wide circle at the bottom. Long ago tepees were covered with deer hides or tule mats and fastened together with a row of wooden pins. Now tepees are made of canvas.

Who do you suppose is going to stay in this beautiful tepee in the woods?

Linda!

Linda's mother and her aunt have brought Linda way up into the mountains. They are going to stay in their great-aunt's tepee while they pick huckleberries. They are going to pick huckleberries on the sunny east slope of Mount Hood.

Linda and her mother and her aunt are in front of the tepee door. Back of them is the straight row of wooden pins that fastens the tepee cover in place. The flaps at the top are open to let the smoke out of the tepee. The fire is built in the center of the tepee floor. Tonight, Linda and her mother will sleep on the ground beside the fire in this tepee.

The River Indians are all leaving the mountains. They are hurrying back to Celilo Falls to fish for fall salmon.

The Chief's wife is coming home from picking huckleberries in the mountains. She has ridden home in this big truck. Chief Thompson does not own a car. He has promised to give a reservation Indian many dried salmon for bringing his family and their dried berries back to the Falls.

The men are hurrying out to the rocks to catch fall salmon. The women are moving their things into the tight little winter houses. Soon they will be making buckskin moccasins and bags to use and sell. When the women are not busy drying salmon and roots and berries and venison, they make beadwork.

The Wy-am-pum long house is east of Chief Thompson's winter home. "Wy-am-pum" means the Wy-am people.

All of the Wy-am-pum meetings are held in this long house. Each spring a three-day salmon feast is held in the long house. It is held to thank the Almighty for sending His People their Great Food.

There is a little carved bird on top of the pole in front of the long-house door. Chief Thompson carved this little bird many years ago. He believes that the spirit of this little bird will carry his messages to the Almighty.

Chief Thompson has the biggest house in the Wy-am village. For many years his winter house had only two rooms. Then Chief decided he wanted a little room of his own. When the babies cry or the women begin talking, the Chief goes into his little front room to think.

Chief Thompson's son, Henry, lives in the little house beside the Chief's winter house.

Linda has been growing all during the summer. Now that the families have moved back to their winter homes, she is too big to stay in her skene. So the Chief's wife has made this little swing for her.

Linda's skene is leaning against the wall. The rattle hoop is turned back over her swing. Linda's mother put it there so Linda would play with her sea shell rattles. But Linda does not want to play with her rattle hoop. She wants to suck her thumb!

The Chief's wife made this pair of little white mittens. She put them on Linda's hands and tied them around her wrists. Linda is still trying to find her thumb. But she will learn that a big girl who has left the baby wrappings of her skene is too big to suck her thumb.

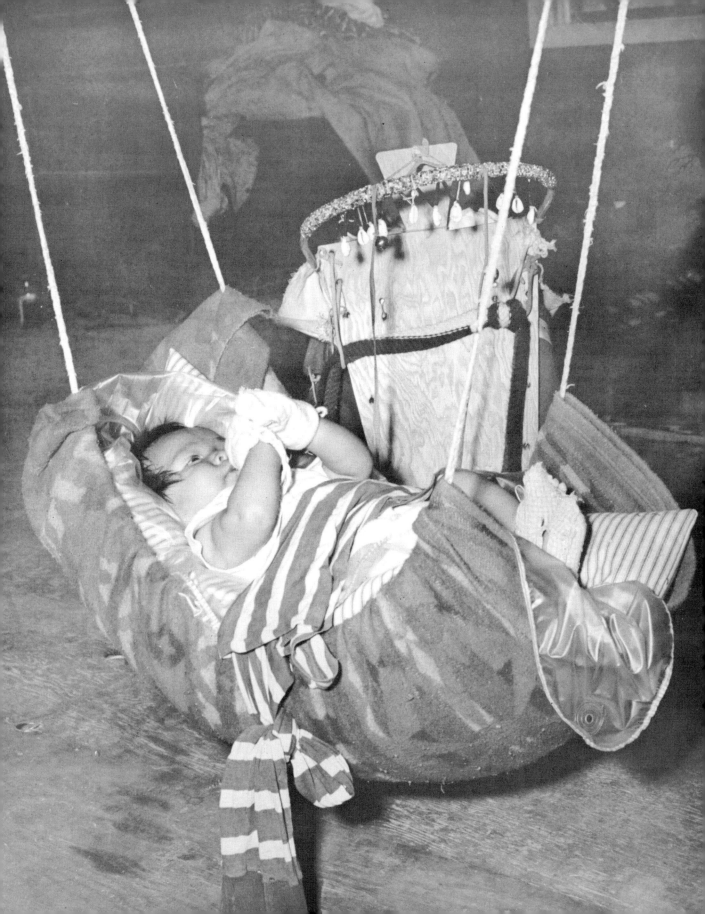

The Chief's wife is combing her hair and watching Linda. Linda is watching the Chief.

When Linda is old enough to talk she will call the Chief "Tee-la."

"Tee-la" is the Indian name for your mother's father — or for your mother's grandfather. "Poo-sha" is the Indian name for your father's father.

Chief Thompson thinks our language is very strange because each child has two grandfathers. He believes it is wrong to call two people the same name.

Because he loves Linda he wants to teach her to follow the Indian ways. The Chief has always believed that the old ways are the best ways for his people. It is very hard for the old Chief to understand white men's words and white men's ways.

Chief Thompson is going to give a memory dinner in the long house. He is giving the dinner so that two Wy-am boys will have happy memories when they leave the village to go into the army.

Chief Thompson tells many stories of the battles his people have fought to help their white brothers. He says his people promised Lewis and Clark that they would always be friends to the white men. Lewis and Clark were the first men from our government to visit the fishing rocks at Celilo Falls. Lewis and Clark brought "the old, old people of the long ago" a message from the Great White Father in Washington, D. C. Chief Thompson is going to tell the story of Lewis and Clark at the memory dinner in the long house.

Mrs. Thompson is braiding the Chief's hair with strips of otter fur. Otter fur is a sign of a chief. Only a great Indian leader wears otter fur in his braids.

The Chief and his wife are ready to leave for the long house. The Chief is wearing his buckskin leggings. He has tied his heavy beaded apron around his waist. He has put on his fringed buckskin shirt and his eagle-feather headdress.

Mrs. Thompson is wearing her blue velvet dress. It is trimmed with elk teeth, beads, porcupine quills and buckskin.

She and the Chief are both wearing "wampum" necklaces. Shell money is called wampum.

The Chief is carrying his pipe of peace. He is carrying his beaded bag. The bag holds his copy of the Middle Oregon Treaty of 1855. This treaty was signed by two Wy-am chiefs named Stoecketli and Ice. Stoecketli was Chief Thompson's uncle. Chief Stoecketli was killed by the Snake Indians. He was killed in a battle while he was helping the white soldiers from Fort Dalles.

Chief Thompson's son, Henry, is called the Sub-chief. When the Chief is away or when he is sick, the Sub-chief acts in the Chief's place.

While he was fishing for fall salmon, Sub-chief Thompson slipped on the rocks and hurt his back. His wife, Black Braids, traded her finest bead bags to get him this bed. He thinks it is very fine to sleep in a real bed, instead of on a mattress on the floor.

Since he has been sick, Sub-chief Thompson and his wife have been making these two dolls. They are a Chief and a Mrs. Chief.

Henry has used thirty-two chicken feathers to make the Chief's headdress. He has trimmed each feather and wrapped it with thread. He says that a woman must never work on a chief's headdress.

Black Braids' doll is wearing two feathers in her headband. Indian women wear two feathers in place of a wedding ring. Two feathers are a sign that a woman is married.

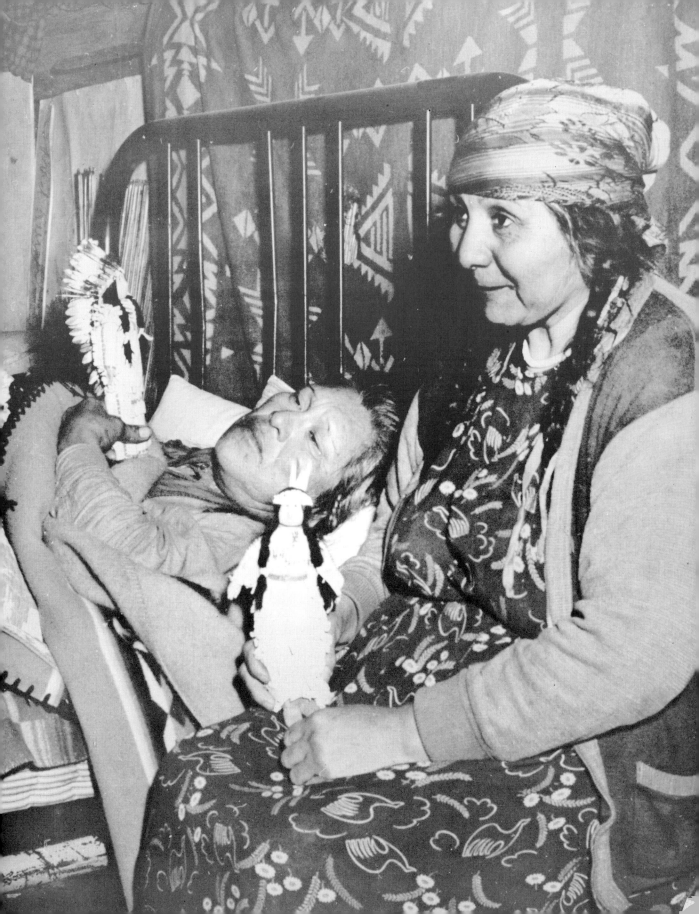

Linda has to stay home. She has chicken pox!

During the night she scratched a big sore on her elbow. So her mother said, "Linda, you will have to wear these little white mittens until you are well again."

Linda is lying on a blanket on the floor. She is listening to the boom-boom-boom of the drums. She is listening to the chanting voices in the big, old, long house next door. She is listening to the roaring river crashing down over the Falls. She is listening to the ringing echoes singing back from the high cliffs. But she is watching her Great-uncle Henry Thompson and her Great-aunt Black Braids finish making their dolls.

Linda hopes to get her hands out of her mittens and onto those dolls. She does not know that her Great-uncle Henry will sell the dolls and use the money to buy groceries.

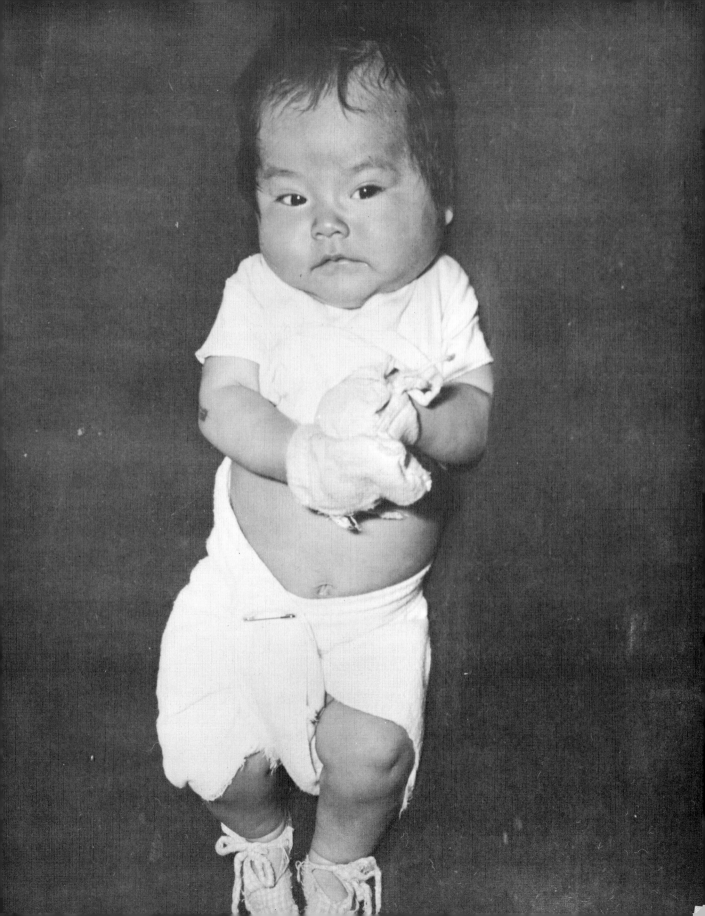

Jimmy George has brought his little girl, Barbara, to the Chief's house. He wants all of the Indians to see her beautiful new white-skinned doll.

This doll was given to Barbara by a kind lady named Nell. Nell often tells stories to little white-skinned children about little red-skinned Indians. One day she came to the fishing village. She saw Barbara sitting quietly in a corner while her mother made moccasins to trade for groceries. Nell said, "I am going to buy that good little girl a doll." And she did!

The Chief's wife looked and looked at Barbara's white-skinned doll. She looked at its white dress. She looked at its white shoes. Then she said, "I am going to buy a white-girl costume for our Linda." And she did!

The Indians all laughed and laughed when they saw Linda dressed like a little white doll. The Chief and his wife were so proud of Linda that they did not worry about spending their grocery money for a little white-girl costume.

Linda is sitting on a blanket in the Chief's house. She is watching the Chief's wife make a beaded belt.

Some day Linda will be big enough to do beadwork too. Maybe she will want to make a story bag that tells of the tepee where she stayed in the woods.

The Chief's wife often carries the big story bag that is leaning against the wall. It shows two elk standing in the woods on a moonlit night. Linda likes to listen to the stories of the beaded bag.

No one has time to tell Linda a story now. Mrs. Thompson, the Chief's wife, is busy. She is making a belt to trade for groceries at the store. Linda does not want to play with the string of big beads the Chief has put in her lap. She is tired of sitting on her own blanket and playing with her own things.

If Linda is not careful she will get into trouble!

She is now reaching for the little piles of beads that the Chief's wife is using. Each little pile of beads is a different color from the others. Each of the colors fits into the pattern she is making. If Linda mixes the beads Mrs. Thompson will not be able to finish the belt today.

The Chief's wife has looked up from her work. She sees Linda crawling toward the little piles of colored beads.

"Linda," says the Chief's wife, "You are a big girl now. You do not live in a skene. You do not live in your own little house any more. You live in a big house with big people now. You must learn not to touch other people's things."

Mrs. Thompson has a low, soft voice. She does not shout at Linda. She does not take her arm and shake her. She does not scold her. She does not slap her. She just looks at Linda like this. She tells her what is right. She tells her what is wrong. She speaks in a kind voice.

Linda listens to her and learns.

Linda is sitting on her own blanket. She is playing with her own string of beads. She is a happy little girl because she is learning to mind.

Linda is learning how big people live in a house together. The Chief's wife is teaching her that it is wrong to take people's time when they have work to do. She knows that Linda will be happier if she does not touch other people's things.

The Chief's wife is almost through with her beaded belt. She can find each color she needs right there in its own little pile on the floor. And she is happy because Linda is happy.

The old Chief is still watching Linda.

He loved her when she was a tiny baby, living alone in her little home in a skene.

He watched her grow. He taught her many lessons.

The Chief is very proud of Linda. He knows that she has learned to live in a big house with big people.

There is love and pride in Chief Thompson's face. He is happy to watch Linda today.

THE END

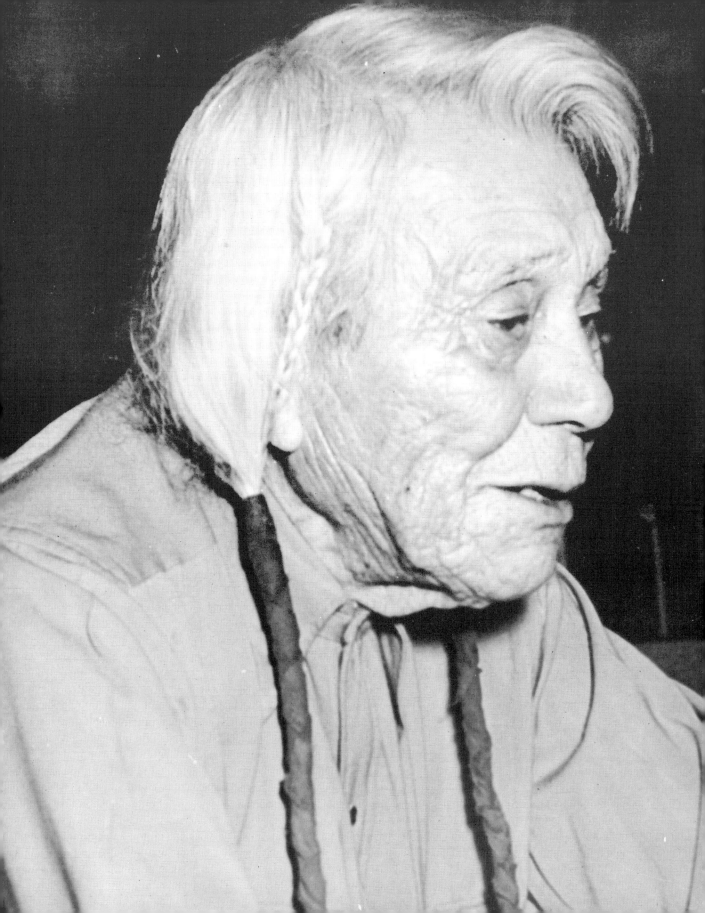

THE WAY THIS STORY WAS WRITTEN:

The Indians at Celilo Falls on the Columbia River like and trust my husband, Archie W. McKeown, who made all of the pictures for this story. They know that when he takes a picture he will give them a copy of it. They know that he sees them as friends and not as dim, shadowy figures, far out on the fishing rocks against a giant backdrop of crashing cataract.

Because I know how much time and patience have gone into the making of his real pictures of real people, I was very happy when one small boy exclaimed: "Them's real Indians. They ain't drawed!"

Here in the deep gorge of the Columbia, I have always had Indian friends, as did my father and his father before him.

It is my honor to be the only adopted, white-skinned daughter of the Wy-ams, who have now lived out their days beside the singing waters of Celilo Falls.

Their stories and legends must not be lost. But their stories were not put on paper for you until Mrs. Marcia Erickson, assistant superintendent of schools for Multnomah County, asked me to tell about my Wy-am friends at a Multnomah County Teachers Workshop. Some of the teachers also told of their need in teaching a required unit on Indian life.

There are many other teachers and inquisitive students who have helped give direction to this story and to the plans for others to follow. Some of them I would like to mention in particular, and by name.

Nell Allen, the library lady of the story, often shares my

journeys to the village at Celilo Falls. David Duniway, Oregon State Archivist, as a visitor in our home, made us aware of the importance of photographic records of this passing civilization.

Among those who read the manuscript, either critically or testing it for school use, are Mrs. Marian Herr, Multnomah County Children's Librarian; Miss Elizabeth Rader, supervisor of elementary education for the Oregon State Department of Education; Miss Helen Schaper, director of curriculum of the Portland Public Schools, and her associates; and Thomas Vaughan, director of the Oregon Historical Society.

The third grade children of the Gresham Public Schools have my appreciation, together with other youthful readers, for pre-testing this manuscript while on its "trial runs."

My thanks go to the faculty and students of the Troutdale Elementary School and the Wy'east High School, where I teach in the Hood River Valley, for courtesies to Chief Thompson and the other Wy-am-pums who appeared at their assemblies and answered their questions.

These courtesies and expressions of sincere interest are, in a large measure, responsible for lifting an age-old ruling against recording the beliefs of the River People.

Most of all I am grateful to my adopted people, the Wy-ams.

I write these words with the full permission of the Chief, who said: "You write, I thumb-print." Here is his signature, Chief Tommy Kuni Thompson, his mark:

MARTHA FERGUSON MCKEOWN
Odell, Oregon,
March, 1956